Taiwan Cookbook

Food from The Streets of Taiwan

BY

Carla Hale

License Notes

No part of this Book can be reproduced in any form or by any means including print, electronic, scanning or photocopying unless prior permission is granted by the author.

All ideas, suggestions and guidelines mentioned here are written for informative purposes. While the author has taken every possible step to ensure accuracy, all readers are advised to follow information at their own risk. The author cannot be held responsible for personal and/or commercial damages in case of misinterpreting and misunderstanding any part of this Book

Table of Contents

Introduction..5

Three Cup Chicken 7

Taiwanese Dumplings... 9

Taiwanese Scallion Pancakes.................................. 12

Taiwanese Fried Rice Noodles 14

Taiwanese Sesame Oil Chicken Soup...................... 18

Taiwanese Fried Tofu 20

Taiwanese Stuffed Beef Scallion Pancakes 22

Taiwanese Oxtail Stew 26

Taiwanese Pork Chops.. 29

Taiwanese Eggplant with Garlic Sauce 31

Taiwanese Pork Buns.. 33

Taiwanese Popcorn Chicken................................... 36

Taiwanese Beef Noodle Soup 39

Taiwanese Beef Stir Fry.. 42

Chicken and Shiitake Mushroom Dumplings 44

Taiwanese Tofu Salad 47

Taiwanese Salt and Black Pepper Chicken 49

Old Fashioned Taiwanese Egg Cake 52

Taiwanese Sa Cha Beef 54

Simple Hot and Sour Soup 56

Taiwanese BBQ Pork Belly 59

Taiwanese Ro Gung 61

Lu Rou Braised Pork 64

Spicy Sichuan Red Oil Wontons 67

Taiwanese Mushroom Soup 70

Conclusion 73

Author's Afterthoughts 74

About the Author 75

Introduction

There is something about Taiwanese culture that is exciting. Without worrying about the politics of the country itself, Taiwan is known for have a unique and distinct culture that has been an influence in various countries around the world. The country is known for being as much of a melting pot as the United States and that can be seen just in the food alone. Embracing trends from Western countries, Japan and South Korea, you will find the food to be made with a variety of ingredients from each of these countries.

That is exactly what you will discover in this cookbook. Inside of this Taiwanese cookbook, you will discover how to embrace the variety of different flavors of authentic Taiwanese foods to make your own delicious Taiwanese dishes in the comfort of your own home. On top of that, you will find 25 of the most delicious Taiwanese dishes that you can make.

So, let's stop wasting time and get straight to cooking!

Three Cup Chicken

This is an easy and authentic Taiwanese dish that is impossible to resist. Best of all, it only takes 20 minutes to prepare.

Makes: 2 to 3 servings

Total Prep Time: 20 minutes

Ingredients:

- 1 pound of chicken drumsticks
- 1 Tbsp. of baker's style baking soda, optional
- 2 Tbsp. of dark sesame oil
- 1, 2 inch piece of ginger, peeled and sliced into thin pieces
- 6 cloves of garlic, peeled
- 1 ½ Tbsp. of soy sauce
- 1 ½ Tbsp. of dark sweet soy sauce
- 1 ½ Tbsp. of Shaoxing wine
- Thai basil leaves, chopped and for garnish

Directions:

1. Rub the chicken drumsticks with the baker's style baking soda. Set aside to rest for 10 minutes. Rinse under running water to rinse off the baking soda. Pat dry with a few paper towels. Set aside.
2. In a wok set over medium to high heat, add in the dark sesame oil. Add in the ginger slices and peeled garlic. Stir well to mix. Cook for 1 minute or until aromatic.
3. Add in the chicken and stir well to incorporate.
4. Add in the soy sauce, dark soy sauce and wine. Stir well to mix.
5. Cover and cook for 5 to 10 minutes over low heat.
6. Add in the Thai basil leaves and stir well to mix.
7. Remove from heat and serve.

Taiwanese Dumplings

If you love the taste of Potstickers, then this is one dish I know you are going to want to make as often as possible.

Makes: 20 servings

Total Prep Time: 3 hours and 15 minutes

Ingredients:

- 2 heads of napa cabbage, chopped
- 1 bunch of cilantro, chopped
- 2 pounds of ground pork
- 2 egg whites
- 3 jalapeno peppers, minced
- 1, 2 inch piece of ginger, peeled and minced
- 1 Tbsp. of sesame oil
- Dash of salt and black pepper
- 3, 16 ounce pack of potsticker wrappers, extra if needed

Directions:

1. On a clean towel, add the cabbage and cilantro. Spread out evenly. Roll the towels around the greens and squeeze out as much of the moisture as possible. Transfer into a bowl.
2. In the bowl, add in the pork, egg whites, jalapenos, minced ginger and sesame oil. Stir well until evenly mixed. Season with a dash of salt and black pepper.
3. Line two baking sheets with sheets of wax paper. Add water into a small bowl.
4. Place one potsticker wrapper into the center of your palm. Add a tablespoon of the pork mix into the center. Dip your fingers in the water and brush the edges to wet them. Fold the edges over and pinch to seal. Place onto the baking sheets. Repeat.
5. Place into the freezer to freeze for 2 hours or until firm.
6. Remove and fill a pot with water. Allow to come to a boil over medium to high heat. Add in the pot stickers and cook for 5 minutes.
7. Remove and serve immediately.

Taiwanese Scallion Pancakes

These flaky and chewy pancakes are so delicious, I know you won't be able to resist them once you get a taste of them. Made with just 5 ingredients, this is an easy dish you can make any night of the week.

Makes: 8 servings

Total Prep Time: 1 hour and 15 minutes

Ingredients for the dough:

- 3 cups of all-purpose flour
- 1 ¼ cup + 2 Tbsp. of hot water
- 6 Tbsp. of water
- 1 ½ tsp. of salt
- ¾ cup to 1 cup of vegetable oil
- 8 to 12 green onions, chopped
- Dash of salt

Directions:

1. Prepare the dough. In a bowl, add in the all-purpose flour and dash of salt. Stir well to mix.
2. Pour in the hot water and stir well to mix until a dough forms.
3. Place the dough onto a flat surface that has been dusted with flour. Knead the dough for 7 to 8 minutes or until soft.
4. Brush the dough with 1 tablespoon of vegetable oil. Transfer into a bowl and cover. Set aside to rest for 30 minutes.
5. Roll out the dough on a floured surface until 1/8 inch in thickness.
6. Brush the top of the dough with 1 tablespoon of oil. Sprinkle the top with a dash of salt. Add the chopped green onions over the top.
7. Roll the dough into a coil shape and place into a baking dish to rest for 30 minutes.
8. Roll out the dough again until 1/8 inch in thickness. Slice into 4 inch triangles.
9. Place a skillet set over medium to high heat. Add in 1 to 2 tablespoon of vegetable oil. Add in the dough triangles. Fry for 2 minutes on each side or until gold. Remove and set onto a wire rack to cool.
10. Serve immediately.

Taiwanese Fried Rice Noodles

This is a recipe that you can make whenever you are craving something simple to prepare. You can find all of the ingredients for this recipe at your local supermarket.

Makes: 4 servings

Total Prep Time: 1 hour and 10 minutes

Ingredients:

- ½ pound of pork loin, thinly sliced
- ¼ cup of soy sauce
- ¼ cup of rice wine
- 1 tsp. of white pepper
- 1 tsp. of powdered Chinese five spice
- 1 tsp. of cornstarch
- 4 Chinese black mushrooms, dried
- 1, 8 ounce pack of dried rice vermicelli
- ¼ cup of vegetable oil, evenly divided
- 2 eggs, beaten
- ¼ clove of garlic, minced
- 1 tsp. of dried shrimp
- 3 carrots, cut into thin matchsticks
- ½ of an onion, chopped
- 3 cups of bean sprouts
- 4 leaves of napa cabbage, thinly sliced
- Dash of salt
- 3 sprigs of cilantro, for garnish

Directions:

1. In a bowl, add in the sliced pork loin, soy sauce and rice wine. Season with the white pepper, powdered Chinese five spice and cornstarch. Stir well to mix. Set aside and let it marinate for 20 minutes.
2. In a separate bowl, add in the dried mushrooms. Cover with water and set aside to soak for 20 minutes. Drain the water and remove the stems from the mushrooms. Slice into thin slices and set aside.
3. In a separate bowl, add in the dried rice vermicelli. Cover with water and soak for 10 minutes. Drain the water and set aside.
4. In a wok set over medium to high heat, add in 1 tablespoon of vegetable oil. Add in the eggs and allow to cook for 2 to 3 minutes or until firm like a pancake. Remove and set aside to cool before slicing.
5. Add in 2 more tablespoons of vegetable oil into the wok. Add in the minced garlic and shrimp. Cook for 30 seconds or until aromatic. Add in the pork with the marinade. Cook for 5 minutes or until the pork is browned.
6. Add in the chopped carrot matchsticks and chopped onion. Cook for 5 minutes or until soft.
7. Add in the bean sprouts, sliced napa cabbage and sliced mushrooms. Stir well to mix. Continue to cook for an additional 5 minutes.
8. Transfer into the bowl with the eggs. Stir well to mix. Wipe the wok clean with a few paper towels.

9. Add the remaining oil into the wok. Add in the drained noodles. Cook for 3 to 5 minutes or until soft.
10. Add in the reserved pork mixture and toss well to mix.
11. Remove and serve with a garnish of chopped cilantro.

Taiwanese Sesame Oil Chicken Soup

This is the perfect dish for you to make whenever you are feeling under the weather. Serve with crusty bread for the tastiest results.

Makes: 6 servings

Total Prep Time: 45 minutes

Ingredients:

- 3 pounds of chicken legs
- 3 Tbsp. of black sesame oil
- 3 ounces of ginger, sliced thinly
- 1, 25 ounce bottle or Taiwanese rice wine
- 3 Tbsp. of rock sugar
- 4 cups of water
- Dash of salt
- 1 scallions, cut julienne style

Directions:

1. Rinse the chicken legs under running water and pat dry with a few paper towels.
2. In a wok set over medium to high heat, add in the black sesame oil and sliced ginger. Cook for 2 minutes.
3. Increase the heat to high. Add in the chicken legs and sear on all sides until browned.
4. Lower the heat to medium. Add in the bottle of Taiwanese rice wine, rock sugar and water. Stir well to mix.
5. Cover and cook for 30 minutes or until the chicken is soft.
6. Season with a dash of salt.
7. Remove from heat. Serve with a garnish of the chopped scallions.

Taiwanese Fried Tofu

This is another delicious authentic Taiwanese dish that you will want to make whenever you are craving something on the healthier side.

Makes: 5 servings

Total Prep Time: 30 minutes

Ingredients:

- 1, 16 ounce pack of extra firm tofu
- 1/3 cup of soy sauce
- 2 tsp. of Chinese black vinegar
- 1 tsp. of sesame oil
- 1 tsp. of white sugar
- 3 Tbsp. of extra virgin olive oil
- 3 cloves of garlic, minced
- ¼ cup of green onions, chopped
- Dash of salt and black pepper

Directions:

1. Slice the tofu into small squares that are ¼ inch in thickness.
2. In a bowl, add in the soy sauce, Chinese black vinegar, sesame oil and white sugar. Whisk until smooth in consistency.
3. In a skillet set over medium to high heat, add in the extra virgin olive oil. Add in the minced garlic and chopped green onions. Cook for 30 minutes or until fragrant.
4. Add in the tofu pieces. Cook for 3 to 5 minutes or until browned.
5. Add in the sauce and toss well to mix. Cook for 3 minutes or until it is slightly thick in consistency.
6. Season with a dash of salt and black pepper.
7. Remove and serve immediately.

Taiwanese Stuffed Beef Scallion Pancakes

These flaky and chewy beef scallion pancakes are so easy to make, I know you will want to make them as often as possible.

Makes: 8 servings

Total Prep Time: 2 hours and 45 minutes

Ingredients for the beef:

- 3 pounds of beef chuck, cut into halves
- 1 onion, cut into quarters
- 5 cloves of garlic, bruised
- 1, 1 inch piece of ginger, thinly sliced
- 4 green onions, cut into 3 inch sized pieces
- 2 carrots, thinly sliced
- 1 daikon, thinly sliced
- ½ cup of soy sauce
- ½ cup of soy paste
- ¼ cup of tomato paste
- 1 Tbsp. of caramel sauce
- 2 Tbsp. of white sugar
- ¼ tsp. of powdered five spice
- 6 cups of water
- Dash of salt and white pepper
- 2 hothouse cucumbers, thinly sliced and for serving
- 8 scallion pancakes

Ingredients for the herb bag:

- 1 star anise
- 1 stick of cinnamon
- 2 bay leaves
- 2 dried chilies
- 2 tsp. of fennel seeds
- 1 tsp. of black peppercorns
- 1 tsp. of cumin seeds
- 1 tsp. of coriander seeds

Ingredients for the sauce:

- 3 Tbsp. of hoisin sauce
- 3 Tbsp. of oyster sauce
- 1 ½ Tbsp. of soy sauce
- 1 ½ Tbsp. of honey
- ¾ Tbsp. of rice vinegar
- 1 Tbsp. of water

Directions:

1. Prepare the beef filling. In a stockpot set over medium to high heat, add in the beef chuck and the remaining ingredients for the beef except for the cucumbers, scallion pancakes, salt and black pepper. Stir well to mix.
2. In a small pouch, add in the ingredients for the herbs. Secure with kitchen twine and place into the stockpot.
3. Cook over high heat and allow to come to a boil. Cover and lower the heat to low. Cook for 45 minutes. Season with a dash of salt and white pepper.
4. Continue to cook for 2 hours or until the beef is soft.
5. Remove the beef from the broth and set aside to cool before shredding finely with two forks.
6. In a bowl, add in all of the ingredients for the sauce. Whisk until smooth in consistency.
7. Brush the sauce onto the scallion pancakes. Top off with the thinly sliced cucumbers, shredded beef and another layer of sauce. Roll tightly and repeat with the remaining pancakes.
8. Slice in half and serve immediately.

Taiwanese Oxtail Stew

Make this delicious oxtail stew recipe whenever you want to spoil your friends and family with something especially filling. The ingredients needed to make this dish are so simple, you can make this dish in just a few hours.

Makes: 6 servings

Total Prep Time: 4 hours and 5 minutes

Ingredients:

- 2 Tbsp. of vegetable oil
- 3 pounds of beef oxtail
- 2 Tbsp. of all-purpose flour
- 2 tomatoes, cut into small cubes
- ½ cup of red wine
- 5 cups of water, or as much as needed
- 1 yellow onion, cut into small pieces
- 1 tomato, chopped
- 3 carrots, cut into small pieces
- 1, 14 ounce can of beef broth
- 2 Tbsp. of soy sauce
- 3 Tbsp. of tomato paste

Directions:

1. In a pot oven set over medium to high heat, add in the vegetable oil. Dredge the oxtails in the all-purpose flour until coated. Transfer into the Dutch oven and cook for 8 to 10 minutes or until browned.
2. Add in the chopped tomatoes, red wine and as much water as needed to cover the oxtails. Stir gently to mix.
3. Allow to come to a boil. Lower the heat to low. Cook for 3 hours, adding in additional water if needed.
4. Place a skillet set over medium to high heat. Add in 1 tablespoon of oil. Add in the chopped onions. Cook for 8 to 10 minutes or until soft. Add in the chopped tomatoes and carrot pieces. Stir well to mix and cook for an additional 3 minutes.
5. Add in the beef broth, soy sauce and tomatoes paste. Stir gently to mix and allow to come to a boil. Transfer into the oxtail mix. Continue to cook for another 20 minutes.
6. Remove and serve immediately.

Taiwanese Pork Chops

Make this delicious Taiwanese dinner dish whenever you are craving something on the filling side. Serve with fried rice for the tastiest results.

Makes: 4 servings

Total Prep Time: 1 hour and 10 minutes

Ingredients for the pork:

- 4 pork chops, boneless, trimmed and pounded to ¼ inch in thickness
- Cornstarch, for dredging

Ingredients for the marinade:

- 2 green onions, chopped
- 4 cloves of garlic, minced
- 2 ½ Tbsp. of soy sauce
- 1 ½ Tbsp. of cane sugar
- ¼ to ½ tsp. of powdered Chinese five spice
- Dash of salt and black pepper

Directions:

1. In a bowl, add in all of the ingredients for the pork and marinade except for the cornstarch. Stir well to evenly mix.
2. Cover and set aside to marinate for 1 hour.
3. In a wok set over medium to high heat, add in 1 tablespoon vegetable oil. Remove the pork from the marinade and dredge on all sides in the cornstarch. Place into the wok. Cook for 3 to 5 minutes or until cooked through.
4. Remove and set aside to rest for 5 minutes before serving.

Taiwanese Eggplant with Garlic Sauce

This is a delicious and mildly spicy dish that I know you won't be able to resist. One bite and I know you will want to make it as often as possible.

Makes: 6 servings

Total Prep Time: 25 minutes

Ingredients:

- 3 Tbsp. of canola oil
- 4 Chinese Eggplants, cut into halves and sliced into 1 inch pieces
- 1 cup of water
- 1 Tbsp. of crushed red pepper flakes
- 3 Tbsp. of powdered garlic
- 5 tsp. of white sugar
- 1 tsp. of cornstarch
- 2 Tbsp. of soy sauce
- 2 Tbsp. of oyster sauce

Directions:

1. In a skillet set over medium to high heat, add in the canola oil. Add in the eggplant pieces and cook for 5 minutes or until soft.
2. Add in the water, crushed red pepper flakes and powdered garlic. Stir well to mix. Cover and cook for 3 minutes or until the water is absorbed.
3. In a bowl, add in the white sugar, cornstarch, soy sauce and oyster sauce. Stir well until dissolved. Pour into the skillet. Toss well to coat.
4. Cook for 5 minutes or until thick in consistency.
5. Remove and serve immediately.

Taiwanese Pork Buns

These pork buns are authentic as Taiwanese dishes can get.
They make for a delicious snack or a light meal any night
of the week.

Makes: 15 servings

Total Prep Time: 3 hours and 30 minutes

Ingredients for the filling:

- 1 pound of ground pork
- ½ pound of green onion, chopped
- 1 Tbsp. of ginger, minced
- 6 Tbsp. of soy sauce
- 4 Tbsp. of oyster sauce
- 6 Tbsp. of sesame seed oil
- 3 Tbsp. of rice wine
- 2 tsp. of white pepper

Ingredients for the pork buns:

- 4 ½ cups of all-purpose flour
- 2 ¼ tsp. of yeast
- 4 Tbsp. of white sugar
- 1/8 tsp. of salt
- 1 cup of warm water
- 4 Tbsp. of canola oil

Directions:

1. In a bowl, add in all of the ingredients for the filling. Stir well to mix. Cover and set into the fridge for later use.
2. In a separate bowl, add in the all-purpose flour, yeast, white sugar and dash of salt. Stir well until evenly mixed. Add in the water and stir gently until a dough forms.
3. Cover and set aside to rest for 10 minutes.
4. Add in the canola oil and knead the dough for 10 minutes or until smooth in consistency.
5. Cover the dough again and set aside to rest for 1 hour.
6. Punch down the dough and place onto a flat surface. Separate the dough into 15 pieces. Roll each piece into a circle that is 4 inches in diameter.
7. In each circle, add ½ cup of the filling. Lift the edges over the filling and pinch to seal. Repeat with the remaining buns.
8. Place the pork buns onto a bamboo steamer and place onto a baking sheet. Cover and set aside to rest for 40 minutes.
9. In a pot set over medium to high heat, fill with water and allow to come to a boil. Place the buns over the steaming water. Steam for 20 minutes.
10. Remove from heat and cool for 5 minutes before serving.

Taiwanese Popcorn Chicken

This is the perfect dish to make whenever you need to satisfy those picky eaters in your own home. It is so delicious, I guarantee they will be begging you for seconds.

Makes: 6 to 8 servings

Total Prep Time: 30 minutes

Ingredients:

- 1 pound of chicken, boneless, skinless and cut into small pieces
- 1 ½ Tbsp. of low sodium soy sauce
- 3 Tbsp. of Shaoxing wine
- 1 Tbsp. of toasted sesame oil
- 1 Tbsp. of dark brown sugar
- 1 Tbsp. of powdered Chinese five spice, evenly divided
- 1 tsp. of white pepper, evenly divided
- 5 cloves of garlic, chopped
- ¼ cup of cornstarch
- 1 egg yolk, beaten
- 1 cup of brown rice flour
- Canola oil, for frying
- Dash of powdered chili, for garnish
- 2 tsp. of salt
- 1 bunch of Thai basil, for garnish

Directions:

1. In a bowl, add in the chicken pieces, soy sauce, Shaoxing wine, sesame oil, white sugar, half of the powdered Chinese five spice, half of the white pepper and chopped garlic. Stir well to mix. Cover and set aside to marinate for 30 minutes.
2. In a bowl, add in the cornstarch and egg yolk. Add into the chicken and toss well to mix. Place the white flour onto a plate.
3. Add the chicken onto the plate with the flour and dredge on all sides. Set aside to rest for 5 minutes.
4. In a pot set over medium to high heat, add in 1 inch of the canola oil. Heat the oil until it reaches 375 degrees. Add in the chicken and cook for 5 to 8 minutes or until golden. Transfer onto a plate lined with paper towels.
5. Season the cooked chicken with a dash of salt.
6. Add the basil leaves to the oil. Fry for 30 minutes. Transfer onto the plate with the chicken and toss well to mix.
7. Serve immediately.

Taiwanese Beef Noodle Soup

This is a delicious soup recipe you can make whenever you are feeling under the weather. Serve on the coldest winter days for the best results.

Makes: 6 servings

Total Prep Time: 1 hour and 20 minutes

Ingredients for the base:

- 3 pounds of beef shank, cut into large pieces
- Vegetable oil, for cooking
- 3 tsp. of light brown sugar
- 1 onion, peeled and cut into halves
- 8 stalks of green onions, cut into halves
- 1, 3 inch piece of ginger
- 2 star anise
- 4 bay leaves
- 4 cups of water
- 1 cup of low sodium beef broth
- 2 Tbsp. of rice wine vinegar
- 1 pound of Asian noodles

Ingredients for the seasonings:

- 3 Tbsp. of Chinese bean paste
- 2 Tbsp. of Taiwan barbecue sauce
- 2 Tbsp. of tomato paste
- 1 cup of Chinese rice wine

Ingredients for the garnish:

- 2 stalks of green onions, chopped
- 2 cups of Asian mustard greens, chopped roughly

Directions:

1. In a large pot set over medium to high heat, add in the beef shank pieces. Cook for 8 to 10 minutes or until browned. Then remove and set the beef shanks aside.
2. In the same pot, add in the onions and in a tablespoon or two of the vegetable oil. Cook for 5 minutes until browned.
3. Add in the star anise, green onions, ginger and bay leaves. Cook for an additional 5 minutes or until aromatic.
4. Add in all of the ingredients for the seasonings. Stir well to evenly mix. Cook for 2 minutes.
5. Add the cooked beef shanks back into the pot along with the water, low sodium beef brother and rice vinegar. Stir well to mix. Lower the heat to low and cook for 1 ½ to 2 hours or until the beef shanks are soft.
6. Transfer the beef shanks onto a plate. Strain the broth through a fine sieve into a bowl. Toss out the solids.
7. Cook the Asian noodles until soft.
8. In serving bowls, add in the Asian noodles. Top off with the cooked beef shanks and pour the strained broth over the top. Serve immediately.

Taiwanese Beef Stir Fry

This is such a delicious stir-fry dish, you will never order Taiwanese takeout ever again. For the best results, serve this dish with steamed or fried rice.

Makes: 4 servings

Total Prep Time: 35 minutes

Ingredients:

- 7 ounces of instant noodles
- 1 Tbsp. of extra virgin olive oil
- 8 ounces of sirloin beef, thinly sliced
- 6 ounces of broccoli, chopped into florets
- 8 ounces of button mushrooms, chopped
- 2 pieces of carrots, chopped finely

Ingredients for the sauce:

- 3 Tbsp. of oyster sauce
- 1/3 cup of low sodium soy sauce
- 1 Tbsp. of ginger, shredded
- 2 cloves of garlic, crushed
- 1 Tbsp. of light brown sugar, packed
- 1 tsp. of sesame oil
- ¼ tsp. of black pepper
- ¼ tsp. of red pepper

Directions:

1. First prepare the instant noodles according to the directions on the package. Drain the noodles and set aside.
2. In a bowl, add in all of the ingredients for the sauce. Whisk well until smooth in consistency. Set aside.
3. In a skillet set over medium to high heat, add in the olive oil. Add in the beef. Cook for 8 minutes or until brown.
4. Add in the chopped button mushrooms, chopped broccoli florets and chopped carrots. Stir well to evenly mix. Cook for 5 minutes or until soft.
5. Add in the drained noodles and toss well to mix.
6. Pour in the sauce. Stir well to evenly mix. Cook for an additional minute or until piping hot.
7. Remove from heat and serve immediately.

Chicken and Shiitake Mushroom Dumplings

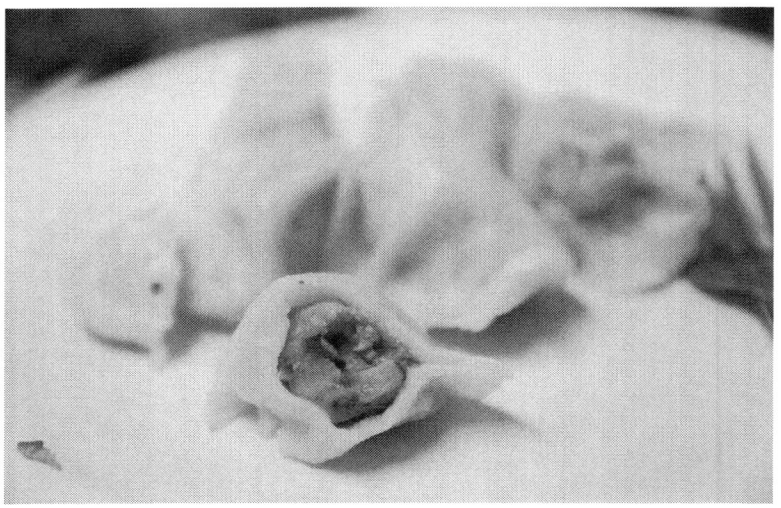

If you need to make a dish that will impress your friends and family during your next lunch or dinner event, then this is the perfect recipe for you to prepare.

Makes: 48 servings

Total Prep Time: 3 hours and 30 minutes

Ingredients:

- 3 1/3 cups of all-purpose flour
- 1 cup of water
- 2 Tbsp. + Tbsp. of vegetable oil
- 1 onion, chopped
- 4 ounces of shiitake mushrooms
- 6 shiitake mushrooms, chopped
- 1 pound of ground chicken
- 2 tsp. of sesame oil
- 3 Tbsp. of soy sauce
- 1 tsp. of white sugar
- 2 Tbsp. of Shaoxing wine

Directions:

1. In a bowl add the all-purpose flour. Gently add in the water and knead gently until a dough forms. Cover and set aside to rest for 1 hour.
2. In a skillet set over medium to high heat, add in 2 tablespoons of vegetable oil. Add in the onion and cook for 5 minutes or until translucent.
3. Add in the chopped mushrooms. Continue to cook for 10 minutes. Transfer the mixture into a bowl.
4. In the bowl, add in the chicken, sesame oil, soy sauce, white sugar, Shaoxing wine and 3 tablespoons of vegetable oil. Stir well until evenly mixed.
5. Divide the rested dough into 48 pieces. Roll each piece until it forms a circle that is 3 ½ inches in diameter. Fill with 2 tablespoons of the filling. Roll the dough over the filling. Pleat the edges to seal. Repeat.
6. Place the dumplings onto a baking sheet lined with a sheet of parchment paper.
7. In a skillet set over medium to high heat, add in 1 tablespoon of vegetable oil. Add in the dumpling and cook for 5 minutes or until crispy.
8. Remove and serve immediately.

Taiwanese Tofu Salad

This is the perfect salad dish for you to make whenever you are craving something on the lighter side. Made with fresh Thai peppers that give this salad a special kick.

Makes: 2 servings

Total Prep Time: 5 minutes

Ingredients:

- 1, 16 ounce block of silk tofu
- Coriander leaves, chopped and for garnish
- 1 green onion, chopped

Ingredients for the seasoning:

- 1 Tbsp. of soy sauce
- 1 Tbsp. of sesame oil
- 1 Tbsp. of water
- 1 tsp. of black vinegar
- 2 Thai peppers, chopped
- ½ Tbsp. of white sesame seeds
- ½ tsp. of white sugar
- 1 clove of garlic, chopped
- 1 tsp. of ginger, minced
- 1 green onion, chopped
- 2 to 3 coriander leaves, chopped

Directions:

1. Chop the silk tofu into small pieces. Set aside.
2. In a bowl, add in all of the ingredients for the seasoning. Stir well to mix and set aside for 2 minutes.
3. In a separate bowl, add the tofu pieces. Pour the seasoning mix over the top and toss well to coat.
4. Serve immediately with a garnish of the coriander leaves and chopped green onions.

Taiwanese Salt and Black Pepper Chicken

There is no other Taiwanese dish that is as simple to make as this one. Made with just a few ingredients and makes for a delicious dinner any night of the week.

Makes: 3 servings

Total Prep Time: 50 minutes

Ingredients:

- 2 chicken thighs, boneless
- 2/3 cup of sweet potato starch
- 1 bunch of basil, chopped
- Vegetable oil, for frying

Ingredients for marinating:

- 1 ½ Tbsp. of soy sauce
- 1 Tbsp. of beer
- 1/8 tsp. of powdered Chinese five spice
- 3 cloves of garlic, grated
- 1 egg
- 1 tsp. of white pepper
- 1 Tbsp. of white sugar
- 2 tsp. of salt

Ingredients for the seasonings:

- 1 Tbsp. of white pepper
- ½ tsp. of powdered Chinese five spice
- 2 tsp. of salt
- ¼ tsp. of powdered curry

Directions:

1. in a bowl, add in all of the ingredients for the marinade. Stir well to mix. Add in the chicken thighs and toss well to mix.
2. Cover and set aside to marinate for 1 hour.
3. Add in half of the flour and stir well to mix.
4. In a wok set over medium heat, add in 2 to 3 tablespoons of vegetable oil. Once the oil reaches 300 degrees, dredge the chicken pieces in the remaining flour. Place into the wok and cook for 5 minutes or until gold. Transfer onto a plate and set aside.
5. Heat the oil until it reaches a temperature of 200 degrees. Add in the chopped basil and cook for 30 seconds. Add in the chicken pieces and continue to fry for 30 seconds. Remove and set aside.
6. In a skillet set over low to medium heat, add in the ingredients for the seasonings. Toast for 1 minute or until aromatic.
7. Sprinkle the seasoning and beer over the top of the chicken. Serve immediately.

Old Fashioned Taiwanese Egg Cake

This is a perfect Taiwanese dish that you can make whenever you are craving something on the sweeter side.

Makes: 12 servings

Total Prep Time: 30 minutes

Ingredients:

- 2 eggs, beaten
- ½ cup of cake flour
- 3 Tbsp. + 1 tsp. of castor sugar
- ¾ tsp. of vegetable oil
- Warm water, as needed

Directions:

1. Preheat the oven to 350 degrees.
2. In a bowl, fill 1/3 of the way with warm water. Add in the beaten eggs and castor sugar. Beat with an electric mixer until fluffy in consistency.
3. Gently add in the cake flour. Continue to beat until smooth in consistency.
4. Add paper liners to a miniature muffin pan. Fill ¾ of the way with the batter.
5. Place into the oven to bake for 15 to 20 minutes.
6. Remove and cool for 10 minutes before serving.

Taiwanese Sa Cha Beef

This is an authentic Taiwanese that is made with beef and served over a bed of cooked rice, to make a filling and simple dish you can enjoy whenever you are craving something exotic.

Makes: 4 servings

Total Prep Time: 30 minutes

Ingredients:

- 12 ounces of beef, thinly sliced
- 1 sweet onion, chopped
- 7 Tbsp. of barbecue sauce
- 5 ounces of baby spinach, chopped
- ½ cup of water
- 1 Tbsp. of vegetable oil
- 2 cups of white rice, fully cooked

Directions:

1. In a skillet set over medium to high heat, add in the vegetable oil. Add in the sliced beef. Cook for 8 to 10 minutes or until cooked through. Transfer onto a plate and set aside.
2. In the same skillet, add in the chopped onions. Cook for 5 minutes or until soft.
3. Add in the barbecue sauce, chopped spinach, cooked beef and water. Stir well to mix. Cook for 2 minutes or until the spinach is wilted.
4. Remove from heat.
5. Serve the beef over the cooked white rice.

Simple Hot and Sour Soup

This is a delicious and restaurant quality soup that you will want to make any time it becomes chilly. Feel free to top off this soup with your favorite toppings for the tastiest results.

Makes: 6 to 8 servings

Total Prep Time: 20 minutes

Ingredients:

- 8 cups of chicken stock
- 8 ounces of shiitake mushrooms, thinly sliced
- 1, 8 ounce can of bamboo shoots, drained
- ¼ cup of rice vinegar
- ¼ cup of low sodium soy sauce
- 2 tsp. of ground ginger
- 1 tsp. of chili and garlic sauce
- ¼ cup of cornstarch
- 2 eggs, beaten
- 8 ounces of firm tofu, cut into small cubes
- 4 green onions, thinly sliced
- 1 tsp. of toasted sesame oil
- Dash of salt and black pepper

Directions:

1. Set aside ¼ cup of the chicken stock for later use.
2. In a stockpot set over medium to high heat, add in 7 ¾ cups of the chicken stock, thinly sliced shiitake mushrooms, can of drained bamboo shoots, vinegar, soy sauce, ground ginger and chili and garlic sauce. Stir well to mix. Allow to come to a simmer.
3. In the bowl with the reserved ¼ cup of chicken stock and cornstarch. Whisk until smooth in consistency. Pour into the stockpot. Stir well to incorporate. Cook for 1 minute or until thick in consistency.
4. Stir the soup gently in a circular motion and slowly drizzle in the eggs.
5. Add in the tofu, sliced green onions and sesame oil. Season with a dash of salt and black pepper.
6. Remove from heat. Serve immediately with a garnish of sliced green onions.

Taiwanese BBQ Pork Belly

One bite of this dish and I guarantee your friends and family will be rushing to grab seconds. It is perhaps the best barbecue pork recipe you will ever find.

Makes: 3 servings

Total Prep Time: 45 minutes

Ingredients:

- 1 pound of pork belly, skinless and cut into strips
- 2 Tbsp. of garlic, chopped

Ingredients for the sauce:

- 2 piece of Chinese red bean curd, fermented
- 1 Tbsp. of honey
- 1 Tbsp. of Chinese Shaoxing wine
- 1 Tbsp. of soy sauce
- 1 Tbsp. of oyster sauce
- 1 tsp. of dark soy sauce
- 1 tsp. of powdered Chinese five spice
- ¼ tsp. of white pepper
- 3 ½ ounces of white sugar

Directions:

1. In a bowl, add in all of the ingredients for the sauce. Stir well to mix. Add in the pork belly and chopped garlic. Stir well to mix. Cover and set aside to marinate overnight.
2. The next day preheat the oven to 400 degrees.
3. Remove the pork from the marinade and place onto a wire rack set on a baking sheet. Place into the oven to bake for 15 minutes.
4. Remove and flip the pork. Brush the marinade over the pork.
5. Place back into the oven to bake for 15 minutes or until fully cooked through.
6. Remove and serve immediately.

Taiwanese Ro Gung

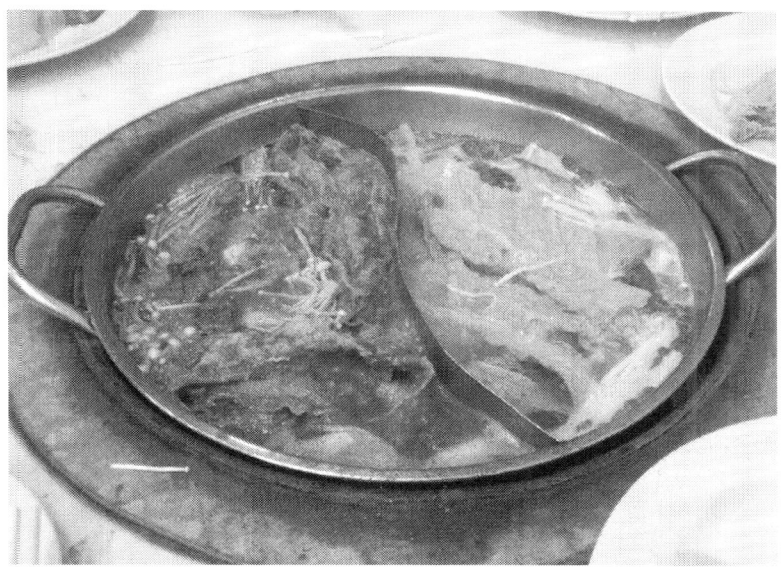

This is a lesser known Taiwanese dish, but it is all the more delicious. It is another soup dish you can make whenever you are feeling under the weather.

Makes: 10 to 12 servings

Total Prep Time: 1 hour

Ingredients:

- 5 dried shiitake mushrooms, thinly sliced
- 7 to 8 ounces of bamboo shoots
- 6 Tbsp. of cornstarch
- 1 ½ pounds of fish paste
- 3 Tbsp. of garlic, evenly divided
- 9 ounces julienne daikon
- 1 pound of pork strips
- ½ cup + 2 Tbsp. of Worcestershire sauce, evenly divided
- 3 Tbsp. of white sugar
- 2 Tbsp. of salt, evenly divided
- 1 Tbsp. of sesame oil
- 1 tsp. of white pepper
- Cilantro, chopped, for garnish and optional
- Steamed white rice, for serving and optional

Directions:

1. Add the shiitake mushrooms into a bowl. Cover with the warm water. Set aside and let it soak for 30 minutes. Drain and slice thinly. Set aside for later use.
2. Peel the bamboo shoots into thin strips. Set aside.
3. In a bowl, add in the cornstarch with 5 tablespoons of water. Whisk until smooth in consistency. Set this mixture aside.
4. In a pot, add in 3 ½ quarts of water. Allow to come to a boil. Add in the daikon and boil for 10 minutes or until soft.
5. In a bowl, add in the fish paste and fried garlic. Add in the pork and stir well to incorporate. Set aside for later use.
6. In the pot, add in the ½ cup of Worcestershire sauce, white sugar and salt. Stir well to mix. Add in the fish paste mix and stir well to mix.
7. Add in the fried garlic, thinly sliced mushrooms and bamboo strips. Stir well to mix and allow to come to a boil. Lower the heat to low. Add in the strips of coated pork gently. Add in the remaining fish paste mix and stir gently to incorporate.
8. Add in the sesame oil and white pepper. Season with a dash of salt. Continue to cook for 15 minutes.
9. Remove from heat. Serve with a garnish of cilantro and the steamed white rice on the side.

Lu Rou Braised Pork

This is a delicious and comforting Taiwanese dish that I know the entire family will love. It is so delicious, I guarantee that nobody will be able to resist.

Makes: 8 servings

Total Prep Time: 1 hour and 30 minutes

Ingredients:

- 2 ¼ pounds of pork belly
- 4 shallots, peeled and thinly sliced
- 1 cup of vegetable oil
- 6 dried shiitake mushrooms
- 1 ½ Tbsp. of rock sugar
- 4 Tbsp. of light soy sauce
- 3 Tbsp. of thick soy paste
- 4 Tbsp. of Shaoxing Wine
- 4 hard boiled eggs, shells removed
- 4 to 5 cloves of garlic, thinly sliced
- ¼ tsp. of white pepper
- 2 green onions, thinly sliced
- 2 to 3 trees of bok choy

Ingredients for the spices:

- 4 star anise, whole
- 2 bay leaves
- 10 Sichuan peppercorns, optional
- 1/8 tsp. of cumin seeds, optional
- 1 slice of ginger, optional

Directions:

1. Slice the pork belly into small pieces
2. In a wok set over medium to high heat, add in 1 cup of the vegetable oil. Add in the sliced shallots and cook for 5 minutes or until gold. Transfer into a bowl and set aside.
3. With 1 tablespoon of the oil left in the wok, add in the pork belly pieces. Cook for 5 to 10 minutes or until light brown. Remove and transfer into a large pot.
4. In the pot, add in the wine, light soy sauce, soy paste, slices of garlic, whole star anise, bay leaves, Sichuan peppercorns, cumin seeds, slice of ginger, rock sugar, white pepper, sliced scallions and chopped mushrooms. Stir well to mix. Pour in water to cover and set over medium to high heat.
5. Allow to come to a boil. Lower the heat to low and cook for 15 minutes.
6. Add in the cooked shallots and hardboiled eggs. Cover and continue to cook over low heat for 30 to 40 minutes.
7. Remove from heat and serve immediately.

Spicy Sichuan Red Oil Wontons

This is another dumpling recipe I know you won't be able to get enough of. This is a versatile dish that you can stuff with your favorite filling.

Makes: 20 servings

Total Prep Time: 25 minutes

Ingredients for the wontons:

- 20 wonton wrappers, square
- 1 bowl of water, for sealing
- 2 to 3 cups of water, for boiling
- White sesame seeds, for garnish

Ingredients for the filling:

- 8 ounces of ground pork
- 2 stalks of scallions, chopped
- 1 tsp. of sesame oil
- ¼ tsp. of white sugar
- ¼ tsp. of salt
- Dash of white pepper

Ingredients for the sauce:

- 1/3 to ¼ cup of soy sauce
- 2 Tbsp. of Chinese black vinegar
- 2 to 3 Tbsp. of Sichuan chili oil
- 1 tsp. of sesame oil
- 1 tsp. of white sugar
- Cilantro, chopped

Directions:

1. In a bowl, add in all of the ingredients for the filling. Stir well to mix and set aside.
2. In a separate bowl, add in all of the ingredients for the sauce. Whisk well until smooth in consistency. Set aside for later use.
3. In the center of each wonton wrappers, add in 1 to 2 tablespoons of the filling mix.
4. Wet the edges of the wonton wrappers with water. Fold over the filling and press the edges to seal.
5. Place the wontons on a baking sheet lined with a sheet of parchment paper.
6. In a pot set over high heat, add in the 2 to 3 cups of water. Allow to come to a boil. Gently add in the wontons. Boil for 2 to 3 minutes or until the wontons begin to float to the surface. Transfer onto a plate lined with the paper towels to drain.
7. Transfer the wontons into a bowl and then pour the sauce on the top. Then gently toss to coat.
8. Serve immediately with a garnish of the white sesame seeds.

Taiwanese Mushroom Soup

This is a vegan Taiwanese dish that every vegetarian or vegan in your home will love. It is perfect to make whenever you want to spoil yourself with something extra special.

Makes: 2 to 3 servings

Total Prep Time: 25 minutes

Ingredients:

- 1 Tbsp. of canola oil
- 1 clove of garlic, peeled and minced
- 2 tsp. of ginger, peeled and minced
- 3 Tbsp. of shiitake mushroom caps, thinly sliced
- 1 carrot, peeled and cut julienne style
- 2 cups of napa cabbage, thinly sliced
- 2 Tbsp. of Taiwanese black vinegar
- ¼ tsp. of white pepper
- ¾ tsp. of salt, extra for seasoning
- 1 cup of enoki mushrooms, cut into halves
- 6 ounces of firm tofu
- 1 cup of vegetable broth
- 2 cups of water
- 4 Tbsp. of tapioca flour
- 2/3 cup of cold water
- Cilantro, chopped and for garnish

Directions:

1. In a pot set over medium to high heat, add in the canola oil, minced ginger and minced garlic. Stir well to mix and cook for 1 minute.
2. Add in the sliced cabbage, shiitake mushrooms, vegetable stock and water. Season with the salt and white pepper. Stir well to mix.
3. Allow to come to a boil. Lower the heat to low and cook for 15 minutes or until the cabbage is soft.
4. Add in the enoki mushrooms and tofu. Stir well to mix and cook for an additional minute.
5. In a bowl, add in the cold water and 2 tablespoons of black vinegar. Add in the tapioca flour and stir well until smooth in consistency. Slowly pour into the soup pot. Stir well to mix and cook for 1 to 2 minutes or until thick in consistency.
6. Remove from heat and serve immediately with a garnish of chopped cilantro.

Conclusion

Well, there you have it!

Hopefully by the end of this book you have found plenty of Taiwanese dishes that you can make from the comfort of your own home. By the end of this cookbook, not only do I hope you have found plenty of new Taiwanese meals that you can make, but I also hope you have gained the confidence to make these dishes regardless of your cooking experience.

So, what is next for you?

The next step for you to take is to begin making all of these delicious Taiwanese dishes for yourself. Once you have done that, it will be time for you to try making your own homemade Taiwanese dishes from scratch.

Good luck!

Author's Afterthoughts

Thanks Ever So Much to Each of My Cherished Readers for Investing the Time to Read This Book!

I know you could have picked from many other books but you chose this one. So, big thanks for buying this book and reading all the way to the end.

If you enjoyed this book or received value from it, I'd like to ask you for a favor. Please take a few minutes to post an honest and heartfelt review on Amazon. Your support does make a difference and helps to benefit other people.

Thank you!

Carla Hale

About the Author

Carla Hale

I think of myself as a foodie. I like to eat, yes. I like to cook even more. I like to prepare meals for my family and friends, I feel like that's what I was born to do…

My name is Carla Hale and as may have suspected already, I am originally from Scotland. I am first and foremost a mother, a wife, but simultaneously over the years I became a proclaimed cook. I have shared my recipes with many and will continue to do so, as long as I can. I like different. I dress different, I love different, I speak different and I cook different. I like to think that I am different because I am more animated about what I do than most; I feel more and care more.

It served me right when cooking to sprinkle some tenderness, love, passion, in every dish I prepare. It does not matter if I am preparing a meal for strangers passing by my cooking booth at the flea market or if I am making my mother's favorite recipe. Each and every meal I prepare from scratch will contain a little bite of my life story and little part of my heart in it. People feel it, taste it and ask for more! Thank you for taking the time to get to know me and hopefully through my recipes you can learn a lot more about my influences and preferences. Who knows you might just find your own favorite within my repertoire! Enjoy!

Printed in Great Britain
by Amazon